THE
- GUIDE -
to people

THE CATS' - GUIDE - to people

Stewart Cowley

illustrated by
Colin Hawkins

NEW ENGLISH LIBRARY/TIMES MIRROR

A New English Library Original Publication, 1981

Designed and produced for New English Library/Times Mirror by
Intercontinental Book Productions Limited,
Berkshire House, Queen Street,
Maidenhead, Berkshire, SL6 1NF.

Copyright © 1981 Intercontinental Book Productions Limited

All rights reserved. No part of this publication may be reproduced or transmitted, in any form or by any means, without permission of the publishers and the copyright holders.

First NEL Paperback Edition November 1981

Conditions of sale: This book is sold subject to the condition that it shall not, by way of trade or otherwise, be lent, resold, hired out or otherwise circulated without the publisher's prior consent in any form of binding or cover other than that in which it is published and without a similar condition including this condition being imposed on the subsequent purchaser.

NEL Books are published by
New English Library Limited,
Barnard's Inn, Holborn,
London EC1N 2JR.

Made and printed in East Germany

ISBN: 0 450 05230 3

CONTENTS

INTRODUCTION

Proud and free, with survival depending entirely on the keenness of your senses and the power of your lean body, you stalk through a wild world where every living creature is prey or mortal enemy and you are lithely, vibrantly alive, a finely tuned instrument entirely at home in a realm of savage beauty.

Almost every cat I have ever known has cherished this image of itself and yearns for its 'lost' liberty. The truth, however, is very different: it is wet out there, and cold. Too often your prey is as keen and agile as you are, and so you shiver through another miserable night beneath a damp hedgerow with hunger gnawing at your belly. When the days are warm there can be no catnaps in some shady nook; there are too many creatures out there to whom you are fair game, so you keep moving, endlessly. Poor and intermittent food, fear, and elements take their toll until one day your senses or your speed fail you and you become the victim of another creature.

How much better to dream glorious dreams in some warm, dry cupboard full of fluffy baby clothes, with your belly full of choice meat and rich milk. There are, of course, disadvantages to living with humans, but they are little more than inconveniences far outweighed by the comfortable way of life made possible. A great deal depends on how you tackle the situation; there is much that can be done to minimize the degree of their interference in your daily routine.

The secret lies in training. The properly trained human can not only guarantee your physical comfort, but can offer you hours of interest and entertainment.

This book takes a close look at these extraordinary creatures, examines their character and behaviour and advises on how to get the best out of your own people. For the beginner, it describes how to choose the people best suited to your needs, and the most efficient means of acquiring them. All their common faults and how to correct them are explained in detail, and even the most experienced cat will find some useful hints and tips that will improve his quality of life.

But human beings have their own needs and problems, so I have devoted some space to this subject, as a happy and fit person is more productive than a morose or ailing one. Remember that once you have chosen your people, they are your responsibility and will become more dependent on you as time passes. Every cat should strive to achieve a relationship that is beneficial to both parties. It will involve a lot of hard work on your part and, at times, disappointment and frustration, but will ultimately amply repay all your efforts.

1.

CHOOSING YOUR PEOPLE

The selection of his very own people is, for any cat, probably the single most important event in his life, making it essential to know a little about how to assess humans. A hasty or ill-informed choice can have long-lasting and unhappy results. Fortunately, unlike ourselves, humans are fairly simple and uncomplicated creatures and it is quite easy to identify basic types.

The characteristics you should be looking for are a gentle disposition, a generous spirit and the ability to respond well to training. These qualities can be found in almost any of the basic types, but are more pronounced in some individuals. This is particularly true of elderly examples, especially female ones past their prime breeding phase. These are often very willing to accept surrogate offspring and will care for you as one of their own. Your fundamental needs will be well catered for, and she will be better prepared to accept any of your whims and fancies than a younger and less tolerant specimen.

Recognising the elderly human

Never attempt to identify a human type by its external coat markings. All humans shed their coats with a most peculiar frequency (as much as two or three times a day), perhaps as a mode of natural camouflage. Look instead for areas of exposed skin which, if well-lined or creased, are a good indication of mature age. One part of the pelt which varies little can be spotted on the head. If this is grey or white, the human is almost certain to be elderly. Inability to move quickly and a certain lack of springiness in the step are also useful clues. Elderly specimens will often be alone, their litters having matured and departed, and this has the added advantage that there will be fewer interruptions to your own daily routine through having to share your new home with her young.

The family phenomenon

The next best category to look for is the human family group, whose members can be identified by their disparate sizes. There will usually be one adult of each sex and it is important, though difficult, to size them up accurately as it is they who will provide most of your facilities.

Analysing a family group

Examine the adults first and look for such clues as the handling of their own offspring. In a descending order of desirability, base your judgement on the following attitudes: first and most suitable; see if they allow their offspring complete liberty of behaviour and are markedly indulgent when the young are loud, boisterous or ill-behaved; also, see if they are attentive to their offspring's desires.

If not of this type, try looking for indications of generosity and attentiveness marred only by a degree of firmness. In some ways this quality can be advantageous to a cat, in that the adults will probably be willing to help you to deal with unwelcome interference by the young. The

disadvantage is mainly that they will also tend to inhibit your own freedom of movement. This is because their firmness is founded on the belief that all should obey them.

The third main type is made up of humans possessing the quality of firmness to a pronounced and, therefore, uncomfortable degree. They will be easily distinguishable by their marked rigidity of posture and crispness of movement. Most telling will be the behaviour of the young, who will be quiet and less prone to bursts of rapid and apparently random movement.

This is usually a sign that the adults' domestic routines are very clearly established and that they will be prone to resentment or unco-operativeness if you disturb them. This can have some advantages: for instance, the provision of your food and other requirements will be taken care of in a predictable fashion which will reduce the amount of training you will need to do.

The independent human

This category is less frequently encountered, but will suit certain cats better than the more common types of human. They often share some of the qualities we possess ourselves and are, in this respect, among the most highly evolved examples of the species. They are unusually independent of other humans, and will only be prepared to accept ownership if relations between you are kept to a minimum. They are unsuitable for cats seeking the optimum in comfort and luxury as they will usually leave you entirely to your own devices, offering only the barest essentials in terms of food and shelter.

They are quite often found on farms or in industrial buildings and are recognisable by their lack of sentimental responses to the usual triggers such as nuzzling and fawning. It is wise to select this type only if you, yourself, wish to live as close as possible to the wild state, but with the security of enjoying guaranteed food and shelter.

Pet shop procedure

For the cat who begins the first stage of his or her life in a pet shop, the opportunity to study your prospective people is severely limited, as you will have little chance to observe them before being faced with a decision. Try to classify them as swiftly as possible, and, if in doubt, reject them. This is quite easily done by staring past them fixedly into space and resisting the impulse to blink until the eyes begin to water. Nestle into a corner and affect an air of listless preoccupation. The occasional sneeze will add to the impression of ill-health, and they should soon leave you undisturbed. If, however, this proves ineffective, spitting, snarling and a few judicious rakes with the extended claws should resolve the matter once and for all.

However, if the people concerned seem entirely suitable and show some initial interest, it is a simple matter to secure them. Buffeting with the head, nuzzling, purring, licking and emitting the odd plaintive mew will make short work of any reservations they may have and you will have found yourself a congenial home.

For cats at liberty or in the wild, the process of selecting a human group is considerably easier and more leisurely. Once you have identified a dwelling that appears of suitable size and location, you will be able to spend as much time observing its people as you wish. Devote a few days to investigating its environment to assess the hunting potential, possible basking-places and so on.

Next, watch the people at work and play until you are satisfied that they will be acceptable. Familiarise yourself with the character of each member of the group, particularly the adult female and any immature young, as these will be the most important factors in ensuring a comfortable life there. Once you have decided to adopt the group, they will also be the ones to work on in order to draw attention to the delights of being owned by you.

Gaining access

The youngest one of the litter is the most useful in gaining access to the house. Wait for a time when it is alone in the garden and approach in a gently playful manner. It will almost certainly be willing to co-operate and will enjoy patting and stroking you. If it is inexperienced in handling you this may cause some discomfort, but until you have been incorporated into the unit entirely, resist the temptaion to teach the young one a lesson. There will be plenty of opportunity later for such reprisals. After a while, the human kitten will probably carry you inside to show other members of the family its new-found playmate, and you can use this opportunity to make a preliminary examination of your new home.

The reaction of other members of the family will range from soft cries of delight at your sweet and gentle disposition, to squeals of alarm at the harm the youngster might have suffered at the claws of a wild animal. The former reaction means that you are home and dry, but the latter poses additional problems, and it will be necessary for you to identify and deal with this adult—who will probably be the mother of the family.

In these circumstances you should, once freed from the grasp of the youngster, make straight for her using the *injured paw limp.* Compounded with head buffeting, sidling, curling the tail around her legs while staring trustingly into her eyes, this should clinch the matter. In extreme cases it may be necessary to adopt the *dragging hind legs* technique, which will make the female assume that to turn you out in that condition is to consign you to inevitable death. At worst, you will be allowed a few days with hot milk and a warm niche in the airing cupboard to recover, and this will be all the time you need for them to abandon any idea of refusing you admission to the family.

Settling in

It will take about a week to establish a basic routine for feeding, etc., after which you can assume that you have been fully accepted and can begin to resume your natural activities. It is also the time when you can begin, carefully and patiently, to train the humans to suit your personal needs. First of all, however, you need to learn the layout of your new home. There are a number of key locations which are important to scout out, and with which you must familiarise yourself.

Somewhere among the ground floor rooms will be one containing a large, fabric-covered object called a settee or sofa. This is used by the humans as a resting-place. As a claw-sharpening site this is ideal. For some reason, this ritual is very exciting to human beings, and they seem to regard it as a signal for play. You will have to choose times when they are absent if you wish to prevent them trying to join in the fun. At first the sofa will seem rather unsatisfactory as a scratching-place, but, after a while, the material will fray and fluff up quite nicely, so always try to use the same spot to work it into the right condition.

Somewhere upstairs will be a particular hiding-place offering warmth and seclusion for those times when you

have had a tiring, wet or muddy excursion outside. It usually takes the form of a cupboard containing a hot water tank and can easily be identified by the soft and comfortable piles of shirts, woollen garments, bedsheets, etc. to be found there. You will be able to make yourself an excellent 'nest' here, but again, do note that humans are often jealous of your diminutive size and will resent your ability to settle in places too small for them. It is an unfortunate character deficiency on their part, that their envy will drive them to expel you from your refuge, so be as unobtrusive as you can when entering or leaving this place.

Sharing Your Home

Your freedom to explore your new residence will depend mainly on whether you have to share the house with any other creatures. If other animals have also taken up residence it is essential that you should establish, as a matter of priority, your rightful place as head of the household.

Dogs

It is astonishing and quite bewildering how many households have elected to provide shelter for that unattractive and unnecessary creature, the dog. Though noisy and excitable they are, fortunately, pretty stupid and easy to subjugate.

A dog will bitterly resent your 'intrusion' into what he mistakenly believes to be 'his' home and you will have to tackle this problem immediately in order to correct the dog's delusion. You should begin by destroying its confidence and air of superiority. This is best achieved by remaining out of sight until the beast is dozing. A lightning dash, a quick swipe at the tender, unprotected nose and the chase is on. Being more nimble and better coordinated you will be able to lead the dog through or around objects which you have already identified as being of some emotional importance to your humans. The dog's clumsiness and awkward bulk will soon leave a trail of destruction through the house for which the unhappy beast will incur the wrath of the humans and be punished accordingly.

Once this process has been repeated a few times, the dog will quickly recognise the futility of competing with you and you will be able to adopt a less energetic approach to sharing the house with it. Do not, however, opt for this technique without having weighed up your opponent beforehand. Some dogs, like terriers or small hounds, are surprisingly agile and may need another approach.

An alternative method is to wait until the humans have prepared some food and left it temporarily on a table. As

soon as they are out of the room, leap up and push it over the edge. The dog, being intensely greedy by nature, will rush in, unable to resist the temptation, and feast on the debris. If the crash of shattering dishes has failed to attract the attention of the humans, a few timely wails and screeches before disappearing will do the trick.

The first two or three weeks are critical, and it is advisable to maintain quite a low profile for this time to allow your humans to adjust slowly to their change in circumstances. Treat them gently and pamper them with your attentions during this time and you will be able to begin the next vital stage of training and conditioning that will ensure both your comfort and their mental and spiritual well-being.

Fish

Humans sometimes keep a fish or two in a bowl of water as an emergency food supply. If you are tempted beyond endurance and succeed in capturing one of these, you may well upset your people, but they quickly recover themselves and forget the incident. They are, however, unlikely to get another fish, so if you wish to have a meal reserved for a rainy day, it is best to leave it alone. This does not mean to say that you cannot practise a little in the meantime.

Birds

Perhaps for the same reason, humans also occasionally keep birds in wire boxes and the above policy also applies to feathered creatures. There is also the possibility that there is some other significance in the presence of a bird, as the humans often devote considerable time in attempting to communicate with them. If you feel that the bird is enjoying a closer relationship with your people than you deem healthy or desirable, lying on top of the cage when the opportunity presents itself is an excellent way of ensuring that the bird will not take advantage of the situation.

The motor car

There is one aspect of your people's lives that is worth special consideration, and it is that extraordinary device which plays such a significant part in their, and therefore your, life; the motor car or automobile. This bizarre entity is easily dominated by even the limited personalities of humans, and serves them as a general 'beast' of burden. Its appearance is awe-inspiring, being encased in an extremely hard and durable carapace within which is a large cavity utilised by humans as a travelling compartment.

An exceedingly ill-tempered beast, it grumbles unceasingly in a most unpleasant and deafening fashion whenever required to serve its masters. Humans are obviously very dependent on its service, as I can conceive no other reason why they would tolerate its constant and disruptive noise, evil odours and unremitting ill-temper.

Perhaps because they somehow recognise our superior intellect and bearing, motor cars are more tolerant of us than are our people, and are quite content to allow us to curl up on their warm hides when the weather permits. Do not expect the same attitude when they are under the control of humans, however, for once this strange battle of wills is resumed, they are quite likely to stampede over you if you are careless about crossing roads. This is simply because they are so preoccupied with bellowing at their occupants that they are particularly unobservant.

I have seen the state of tension between the species reach such levels that it results in physical violence and the human has brought the chastened motor car home bearing the scars of a fierce combat. This can also happen between motor cars which, for one reason or another, engage in battle.

Establishing your authority

One of the first things you will have to do as an owner taking over a new family is to establish, as dramatically as possible, your superior abilities, courage and, therefore, authority. The importance of this cannot be overstated and a strong impression made at this stage will make later training and disciplining very much easier, and will reduce the risk of a reaction against your authority.

Of the several methods of achieving this objective, one of the most effective and commonly employed is the Steeple-jack Ploy which will demonstrate, in a suitably impressive fashion, your strength, stamina, dexterity and fearlessness. First select a suitable tree. (This does not necessarily mean that it has to be the largest; a spindly one of medium-height will do just as well.) Make your way to the top at your leisure, since it is not essential for this part of the exercise to be witnessed by your people.

Once you have reached a suitably elevated position, make yourself as comfortable as you can and start trying to attract their attention. Keep calling until finally one of the group notices you. The reaction is immediate and most gratifying and will evoke loud cries of admiration. Within a very short time, this individual will summon the others to witness your daring and courage, and their reactions will be similarly awe-inspired.

At this point you will immediately be able to single out the dominant member of the human group, and therefore the first one you will have to subjugate to your will. This individual will see your feat as a direct challenge to his or her own authority and will immediately attempt to demonstrate equal ability by emulating your climb. It is quite possible that news of your ability has spread beyond your own people, and others will rush to the spot to witness it for themselves. This will not only reinforce the impression you are making, but will encourage a feeling of pride in your own people that can only strengthen your relationship with them.

Meanwhile, the dominant male will have already either

failed to ascend the tree or will be slowly and painfully working his way up to your position. Keep a close watch on his progress until you are satisfied that he can get no further. If he has actually succeeded in getting quite close, move a little further up the tree and continue to do so until he is finally forced to admit that he is unequal to the task. The required impression of superiority having been made, you can now slip past him and return to where your people are gasping in admiration.

This technique can take a fairly long time, but is well worth it as a means of dramatically underlining your authority right from the start. You may still find that the adult male continues to resent the usurping of his role as head of the family group, but at least a useful start has been made.

As an interesting adjunct to this technique, it sometimes precipitates a most intriguing event. It seems that when an adult male fails to equal your standard, his frustration can be so great that he will try another ploy to prove that you can be beaten, and he will summon an elite group of human height-achievers.

These are easily recognised by the uniformity of their pelts and the fact that they will appear with a huge red motor car equipped with a symbolic tree. This will be extended towards you, and one of these humans will, with verve and confident speed, clamber up the symbolic tree to your vantage point. It is, in such cases, important not to allow your feat to be diminished by allowing him to carry you to earth again, and you should refrain from participating any further and make your way to the ground without further ado.

2.

DISCIPLINE AND TRAINING

The time immediately after your acquisition of a new home is always very exciting; there is so much to see and discover about your future environment. Many cats spend the first weeks either slinking about in an abstracted sort of way, overwhelmed by the whole thing, or dashing wildly round in a frenzy of excitement, thoroughly unsettling their new, and therefore slightly apprehensive, people.

Do remember that this is a critical stage in your relationship with your humans, and it is vitally important that you should establish your domination from the outset. Either of the reactions described above will undermine your position to some degree; you will suddenly seem more uncertain, vulnerable or disorganised than is fitting for one who has undertaken responsibility for a human individual or group. You must not allow your people to doubt your own confidence at any time, particularly at the beginning, so maintain your 'cool' and resist the temptation to rush about shrieking with manic exuberance and the fever of discovery.

Every human household contains a specific area called a kitchen where food is stored and prepared, and this is easily identified by the fact that there is an abundance of cupboards and raised surfaces. Identify this area as quickly as possible, without giving the impression of

unseemly haste, and position yourself in the centre of the room. If you can spot the rectangular metallic cupboard called a 'fridge', seat yourself in front and facing it. Adopt an expression of bored anticipation and refuse to move until your humans grasp that you expect to be given a meal. This will establish the meal requesting pattern in no uncertain way right from the very start.

Some eminent cats consider that it is also advisable to be fussy about the food accepted at this point, but my own view is that it is possible to overstep the mark at this delicate introductory stage. Your humans are entirely untrained at this time, and it is difficult to be certain that they will not become irritated and undisciplined in their reaction to your sudden and unnerving fastidiousness.

Slow but sure

There is much to be said for a gradual period of acclimatisation for them rather than the *shock treatment* recommended by some authorities. Do not forget that, primitive and unsophisticated though they may be, they will have enjoyed complete though unedifying liberty for some time prior to your arrival, and may well feel some initial reluctance to submit to your authority. A firm, but gentler approach, in my experience, usually yields far better and longer-lasting results. It will allow you to turn them away gradually from their customary mindless existence, replacing it by easy stages with a healthier and more rewarding way of life, until they scarcely even remember earlier behavioural patterns.

A general principle for all training is consistency. Once you have determined the best programme for your individual needs, you must stick to it. Change of mind or of tactics are counter-productive and will only confuse your humans and encourage rebellion.

The first step is to make known your requirements and here, as in other stages of training, repetition is the key. Do not get discouraged if, at first your people fail to understand your command and always try to demonstrate your wishes by example or mime. Human beings are simple creatures and are prone to becoming completely involved in their own obscure rituals and customs. This is something that you will have to change if you are to re-educate them. A good starting point, in view of their low intelligence, is the principle of mesmerism.

Using mesmerism

Wait until the human in question has settled down, then position yourself close in front of him. Make sure that you are comfortable, as this will take a little time. Fix him with an unwavering and implacable stare and concentrate your thoughts on reaching deep 'inside' his brain. Do not allow your attention to waver, but focus on an imaginary point in the centre of his skull and resist the temptation to blink or move your eyes. It will only be a matter of minutes before your telepathic presence begins to register.

This is signalled by an increasing restlessness on his part; he will begin to fidget, cough nervously and look up from whatever he is doing with increasing frequency, although he will take pains to avoid meeting your gaze. After some moments he will acknowledge your presence, and you should now advance towards him without taking your eyes away until you are close enough to spring lightly on his lap. Begin a slow, deliberate pumping movement with your fore-paws (keeping your claws in), an action which humans seem to find comforting, while continuing to stare intently into his eyes.

The usual reaction is for humans to surrender to your aura of intellectual superiority and begin trying to please you. In extreme cases they may try to reassert their own authority by pushing you away or onto the floor. It is imperative that you should not accept this response, but should repeat the process, until they finally submit.

At times it will be necessary to assert your authority over them when they are actually engaged in some physcial activity, such as carrying objects from one room to another. The correct technique here is to take advantage of the inherent physical instability that comes from their extraordinary insistence on walking on their hind legs only. Exploiting your own natural dexterity of foot and physical co-ordination, weave swiftly between their moving feet a number of times until they begin to lose their balance and rhythm of movement. This will often be accompanied by raucous cries of alarm as they realize how awkardly they walk compared with you, and sometimes produces the petty reaction of hurling aside the objects they were carrying. If this happens, it is advisable to retire for a few moments until they have collected themselves together once more, and perhaps postpone any further training until another day.

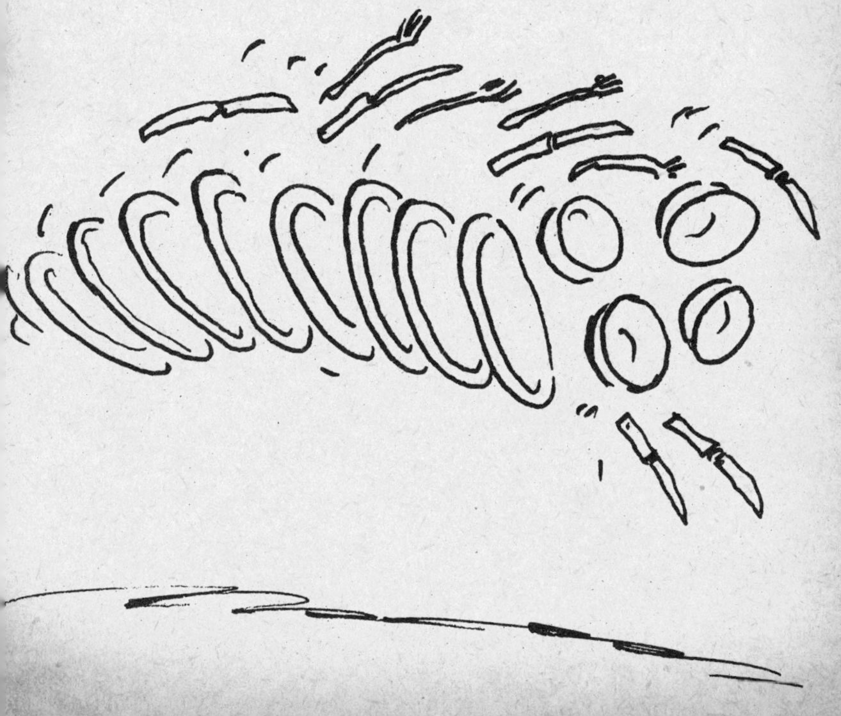

Re-education

Before proper training can get underway you will have to work hard at undoing the many, quite firmly established, behavioural patterns that they will have acquired earlier. You must register a prominent place for yourself in their consciousness. Here, *shock therapy* is often effective in ensuring that you are never far from their thoughts even when you are not actually present.

At night, try curling up next to, or even on top of, their faces, but be ready to spring away once they hurtle upright, screaming and clawing at the air. You will find many of your own opportunities once you are clear about your aim. As soon as you notice a curious, hunted expression in your people, you will know that you have succeeded in placing yourself well to the fore of their minds, and training is well under way.

The reward system

Without doubt, the *reward system* is one of the most effective training techniques you can use. Humans are fairly slow to learn, because of their preoccupation with the intricacies of their own curious life-style. They are easily distracted, and alternate between frenzied activity and long periods of a strange, trance-like state. To learn new behavioural patterns they need constant reward and encouragement to re-inforce the instruction.

Together with the use of punishment (which will be discussed later on), the reward system must be applied sparingly and with forethought. One of the most useful techniques is that of present-giving, which need not be applied only as a reward for a particular response to training. Gifts made spontaneously at intervals help to maintain the close bond of companionship that is so essential to a continuing and mutually beneficial relationship.

The most common method is to present your people with one whole mouse from the previous night's catch, but if this seems too extravagant to you, then a portion of its corpse will usually be sufficient. It is not necessary to make the presentation personally: in fact the act of giving is more effective if understated. The gift can simply be left in a strategic position such as on the doorstep, or in the hall or kitchen. The staircase is a particularly good site as it will then be the first thing they see on descending from their sleeping-quarters in the morning, and will give them a most exciting start to the day.

Humans are incredibly inept at catching their own mice, and, extraordinary though it may seem, often have to resort to the use of small, and, it must be admitted, rather ingenious artificial devices to capture their prey. Because of the great difficulty they have in this area, it is easy to be caught unawares by the nature of their reactions when receiving such a gift. At first sight, there seems little doubt hat they are overjoyed at discovering your juicy titbit—indeed it is inconceivable that this would not be the case. They will appear so excited that they will rush about at an alarming rate emitting shrill, piercing cries, but it seems quite likely that their enthusiasm is not all you might believe it to be.

Experience of human psychology suggests, in fact, that it is not excitement, but fury, that precipitates this type of somewhat excessive response. The sounds and actions of an enraged human are almost indistinguishable from those of a deliriously happy one, and a mistaken assessment can lead to disaster. In this particular instance it is very possible that, where it seems that the human concerned is furious about the appearance of the gift, it is due to a feeling of inadequacy about his or her own lack of success which is exaggerated by the symbol of your own skills.

Even in these cases, however, there is little doubt that the gift is ultimately appreciated as the mice always vanish sooner or later, usually the former, so do not be deterred from performing this important little ritual.

Try to resist, however, the temptation to make such presentations too often. It is easy to run the risk that they

will come to rely on your help too much and will expect a regular supply. For the same reason, do not provide more than one or perhaps two gifts on a single occasion. Attempting to surprise them with a huge pile of stiffening mice will not only exhaust you but will endanger them. Their excitement seems to increase in proportion to the number or size of gifts left at any one time, and too large a heap may precipitate a dangerous excess of passion. You can linger nearby if you wish to witness their reaction to your helpfulness and generosity but do try to remain out of sight. As any human-owner knows, people are huge, heavy, and extremely clumsy. If they see you nearby they are likely to hurl themselves at you in hysterical gratitude, unaware of the physical injury they may inflict on you.

Avoiding complacency

Even when you have succeeded in establishing domination over your people, you will need to remind them of it occasionally to prevent their starting to take your presence for granted. It is very easy to settle into a regular routine where the humans provide you with food and other necessities automatically without really being aware of your existence. To prevent this happening you should employ different techniques to keep them on their toes and attentive to you.

Once feeding-times, door-opening times and other regular events have been well established, a useful variation is to settle yourself in a snug refuge that you have not used before and which is unlikely to be investigated by your people. Provided that you have fed well before your withdrawal, you should be able to stay there for up to 36 or even 48 hours without having to move. At key times when they would normally be performing one of the ritual tasks they have been trained to do they will become fidgety and restless. You will hear them moving about aimlessly, unwilling to admit that they are not happy to be relieved of their duty yet filled with a vague feeling of guilt. This will increase until they become positively alarmed by your long absence. The adult female will probably be the first to break, terrified that you may have abandoned them and left them without an owner. Amid much growling and snarling, the adult male will be dispatched to search outside the house.

A place in the human heart

The following events are most interesting to observe, and will characterise the usual cat/human relationship. The human will feel compelled to assert his own independence by pretending not to care whether you have departed or not, but will secretly be frightened by the prospect of being ownerless and bereft of your controlling influence. This is demonstrated by the apparently careless way he wanders round the garden, irritably calling out to you and poking half-heartedly at hedges, bushes and clumps of tall grass. The true extent of his concern, however, is demonstrated by the length of time he spends, encouraged by the female, plodding round and round the immediate vicinity with occasional lengthy excursions further afield.

As his concern mounts, the growls and protestations grow louder and more continuous until, with the roaring and bellowing of naked fear, he storms back into the house where the adults conduct a raucous and intriguing duet as they seek to overcome their terror of impending solitude. One theory is that this deafening chorus is intended to exorcise the demons that will now be free to enter without the cat to banish them.

This is the point at which you should emerge from your hiding place in as casual a fashion as possible and amble calmly through the room where this curious ritual is being performed to your feeding-place. The female will rush after you and lavish much affection on you, clasping you and piling all sorts of delicacies on your dish. In characteristic style, the male, overwhelmed with gratitude at your reappearance but unwilling to express his delight, will either throw himself into a seat and withdraw into a meditative state, probably behind a large sheet of paper with black marks all over it, or will rush from the house in an excess of joy.

Behavioural aberrations

In this case you will note an interesting phenomenon that occurs with the male of the species at such times. When he finally returns, after some hours, he is often unable to co-ordinate properly, and exudes a curious odour coupled with an air of benign indifference. This may be due to glandular hyperactivity precipitated by extreme emotion on your safe 'return'. This peculiar scent is also apparent at other times, even when the male remains within the family home. It seems to have a dehydrating effect on the human body as the manifestation of the aroma is accompanied by a marked increase in the human's intake of fluids.

There is still a lot to learn about this extraordinary species, and there are certainly times when it is wise to recognise that even a cat may not be entirely safe from irrational and sometimes violent behaviour on the part of humans. The above occasions are cases in point.

Your socio-political function

One of your major roles in the human group is that of peacemaker. As with any closely integrated group of creatures, domestic friction and tension will inevitably arise and you will often be required to help restore equilibrium. In most cases you can afford to refrain from interfering, as these confrontations are usually part of the natural process of establishing hierarchical status. These take the form of an aggressive display between two or more of the group; often either between one of the adults and one of their young who are experimenting with their growing self-assurance, or between the male and the female as a means of reaffirming their relative positions within the group.

Noisy though these may frequently be, they are seldom anything more than a disruptive, but harmless ritual involving verbal threats and symbolic physical aggression such as the hurling of harmless objects. For the resident cat, these displays are irritating and sometimes inconvenient, but must be allowed to take place without interference on your part as they are a vital part of human social communication.

The real dangers lie in the situations where serious and actual antagonism exists. These can be identified by the lack of overt and obvious vocal and physical displays, and most frequently occur at night between adult humans. It is very difficult to anticipate these dangerous confrontations but, by careful observation of their frequency, they can sometimes be found to follow a certain pattern. They most frequently arise after all the humans have retired for the night. The adults settle down in their usual way, and in fact the atmosphere of harmony seems even more pronounced than at other times. Even the most cautious cat can be convinced that all is well, but within a few moments the reverse can suddenly become the case with the two adults locked in silent, merciless combat; a deadly duel conducted with soundless ferocity under cover of the darkness.

The moment you realise what is going on, you must act as swiftly as possible before a tragedy occurs. If the struggle has been in progress for a while you cannot afford subtlety. Enter the bedchamber as fast as possible, and without hesitation, hurtle across the intervening space and launch yourself into the air with a bloodcurdling screech; calculating your trajectory to land you on any exposed area of human anatomy, irrespective of the owner.

The resulting bellow of terror almost inevitably signals the passing of the danger and you can retire knowing that catastrophe has been averted. If, however, you are lucky enough to detect a drama of this kind at the outset, you can adopt a less urgent approach. You can, for example, simply sit on the floor beside the bed, fix the occupants

with an unvarying stare and commence purring, the latter being most soothing for humans. They will soon notice you and will be distracted, allowing the build-up of tension to be dispersed very quickly. As soon as one of the humans rises to remove you from the chamber, make your own way out, calmly and without haste.

There is still the possibility that the situation will not have been entirely defused, so linger outside the door until you are certain that it will not recur. If it does, it will be sufficient if you remain there and mew continuously. One of them will again arise out of concern for your welfare and you can withdraw until they have returned to the bed. Repeat as often as necessary to dissipate the tension entirely.

Punishment

The use of punishment as a training tool should be kept to a minimum, and will be more effective if applied sparingly and objectively, but it is quite likely that there will be a few occasions when there is no real alternative. For example, humans have entirely different notions from ours as regards personal hygiene, and instead of cleaning themselves at frequent intervals throughout the day as we do, choose instead to submerge their bodies, except their heads, in hot water. Why they elect to inflict such an unpleasant experience on themselves is open to debate. There is a strong argument for suggesting that it is a spiritual renewal ritualised in the form of a symbolic return to the womb, or it may be a form of penance.

It is clearly of tremendous importance to them and they are, unfortunately, rather prone to believing that other forms of life, even higher ones, will also benefit from this symbolism. It is not unknown for them to insist, doubtless for the most laudable reasons, on forcibly introducing their cat to this terrifying ceremony. So anxious are they to 'help' their patron in this way that they will use brute force, and there is not much you can do to prevent this happening. All you can really make sure of is that it never happens again, and this is where the judicious use of punishment is, regrettably, inevitable.

The actual form it takes will obviously vary according to he circumstances and the nature of your people, but some suggestions might be useful. It is no use scratching or biting, as you will, no doubt, have employed these direct approaches during the course of the struggle to keep out of the water. Your misguided people will have been prepared for this eventuality and will have steeled themselves to endure physical suffering for its duration. They will, however, only expect it while the operation lasts and will be unprepared for any such ferocity after its conclusion. Psychologically, therefore, this is the best time to strike. Rushing in and out of the room, emitting ear-piercing shrieks of fury, to lacerate exposed ankles and shins, ladder stockings and chew pieces of flesh from careless fingers will do much to ensure that they get the message and make no further attempt to force their own rituals upon you.

Alternatively, you could go for a more subtle approach, such as repairing directly to the adult's bedchamber and sliding your wringing wet and, if possible, soapy body deep inside their bedding, or springing lightly with claws in action on to the piles of dainty undergarments that are often stored in the airing cupboard. This is still more effective if you have previously rushed outside, rolled on the flowerbeds and danced lightly over the compost heap. Using the disappearing technique described earlier, but for a longer period of time, is also quite effective. If you follow this up by hissing at your people for the next few days this will reinforce the learning process.

Do remember when using punishment, however, that humans are of fragile temperament and their mental equilibrium can be irreparably damaged without care in the application of punitive measures. If you insist on hiding above doors or staircases and dropping with extended claws onto the heads of your people too frequently, they are likely to deteriorate rapidly and will eventually become unusable. You will then have no alternative but to acquire a new set, with all the problems of training that this involves.

The language barrier

Human beings possess only a very limited linguistic capacity, although there is little doubt that they are able to communicate among themselves very effectively. Your relationship with them will therefore depend very much on your ability to teach through repetition and example. Be patient and consistent and your efforts will be rewarded.

It is possible to train them to respond to a limited range of spoken commands provided that you keep them simple and speak clearly and firmly. Below are listed a suggested range of command words to cover some of the basic requirements.

EEOWW-YYOWW . . . . I'm quite peckish and my meal is now due.

MMEWWW . . . . I'm unwell/sleepy, and do not wish to be disturbed.

WWRREEECH . . . . . Get off my tail/foot you gigantic lump.

BROOWWRRR . . . . . I've a fat, juicy mouse for you. Come and get it!

MMRRRUUMM . . . . (Spoken on ascending lap) Stroke me.

PURRRR-PURRRR . . Keep stroking me.

This vocabulary will be about as much as the average human can handle. Always use the same tone and inflexions, as they recognise the sound rather than the intrinsic meaning.

3.

THE IMPORTANCE OF PLAY

The advantages of living with human beings are fairly self-evident: a regular supply of good quality food, shelter, and access to a high degree of medical care if required. These benefits, however, do carry with them a certain measure of responsibility which must not be shirked if one is to ensure adequate standards.

As any cat experienced in the art of co-habiting with these rewarding, but frequently exasperating, creatures will verify, the period of initial training and subsequent reinforcement, though essential, is not really sufficient to make the most of their potential. Once properly trained they are fairly consistent and conscientious in attending to your needs, and it is easy to feel that you have done all you should to establish their behaviour patterns.

They are, however, highly emotional creatures and their obscure and very complex activities place them under considerable stress at times. You will notice disturbing irregularities in their emotional state, dramatic changes of pace in their activity levels and, as I have said, curious, trance-like states at frequent and quite regular intervals. The latter are one of the most distressing of these phenomena, and indicate that the human concerned has suffered some sort of emotional overload which has numbed its faculties and produced a state not unlike that

of a coma. During such a period, they usually attempt to find relief by enlisting the help of a device which displays familiar, and therefore comforting, images in quick succession together with an unrelenting wall of random sounds which creates a type of sensory blanket to cocoon them from the unwanted stimuli of the outside world. There has, incidentally, been a theory proposed that the device itself is responsible for this withdrawn state, but this hypothesis fails to explain why they should activate the device in the first place.

As creatures of sensible and relaxed habits, cats will find this intrinsic instability an anathema and, indeed, it is likely to result in unacceptable variations in the desired routine, such as delays in the provision of meals. This raises the vital question of the *importance of play* for domestic humans and, after initial training, is one of the most vital responsibilities the wise human-owner must assume. Though it will inevitably be a tedious duty at times, neglecting this aspect will prevent your humans from realising their full potential.

Dealing with trances

To start with, it is essential that you familiarise yourself with the symptoms of this malaise and begin to recognise the customary patterns. The most usual, and certainly most dangerous is the hypnotic, artificially induced trance described above, but the onset of this phenomenon is fortunately quite easily recognised and can be swiftly tackled. Easier to miss, however, is the paper fixation, which takes a number of forms. The human can adopt any one of several attitudes when about to indulge in this withdrawal, the most usual being that of the chair position.

Here the human will seat itself, often while making a series of sighs or amiable grunts, and will fidget restlessly until satisfied with the position adopted. It will then pick up and manipulate, a collection of large pieces of paper covered in meaningless hieroglyphics. Almost immediately, it enters the trance state described. Except for the occasional grimaces or bursts of random sound the face loses all mobility and the eyes flick from side to side in an alarming fashion indicating a mild form of hysterical spasm. The human is evidently aware enough of what is happening to it to feel some measure of self-consciousness as it will shuffle and toy with the papers at irregular intervals in order to give the impression that it is conscious and unaffected by the mesmeric effect produced by the sheets.

The caring cat must act in these circumstances to prevent the catalepsis worsening, and his movements must be decisive and abrupt. There are two favoured techniques which differ only in detail. The first is to take a position directly beneath the sheets of paper and await the next period of immobility. As soon as the subject has relapsed into the trance, gather the haunches beneath you, get a good grip on the floor-covering and propel yourself up through the sinister sheet with sufficient velocity to pass completely through and onto the chest of the human patient. The result will be electric and utterly effective, but will be accompanied by an enormous volume of noise and physical activity during which you are well advised to vacate the area until the human has recovered from the shock of forcible re-entry into the living world.

The second technique is somewhat more restrained and is better suited to humans less subject to deep trances, and will involve ascending the rear of the chair. If you are uncertain as to the extent of trauma, you can test the situation by purring and rubbing your head against the recipient's neck. This will be enough to distract minor cases but will be answered by irritable responses if the situation is more serious. The next step is, therefore, to position the hind feet on the very edge of the chairback and in one swift and fluid movement, kick the hind feet clear of the chair at the same time as reaching upwards to fasten the front claws into the upper surface of the scalp. As the latter takes the full weight of your body it will initiate a similar response to the first technique described, but your safety is assured by the fact that on releasing the front claws you will drop immediately to the floor and out of reach.

Dealing with minor trances

Other common variations in trance attitudes are those of the table and, frequently adopted by younger humans, the floor positions, which though indicative of the same malady and treated through similar methods do require slightly different approaches for purely tactical reasons. For deviations from these classic situations, you must work out individual solutions yourself bearing in mind the extent of shock-therapy required.

With regard to the latter, it must be stressed that frequency of full treatment must be carefully rationed as it is all too easy to imprint an undesirable form of conditioning in the human concerned. It will acquire an instinctive fear or resentment response which is wholly counter-productive, and results in a marked deterioration in the domestic environment.

A less dramatic approach which can be applied in either the table or floor situations is that of *passive interference* which, in both instances, involves sliding as unobtrusively as possible round the edge of the human's peripheral vision until you are able to step directly and gently onto the outspread sheets of paper. Once in place you should settle yourself into a comfortable position, preferably facing the patient and therefore able to fix it with a direct and tender gaze, and await the breaking of the comatose state. Do not be diverted from this course by the lack of any immediate success. It may take two or three attempts, during which the human will refuse to co-operate and will push you away from the paper, before its reactive potential is sufficient to disrupt the trance. If, however, repeated attempts fail to achieve the desired effect, it will become necessary to consider adopting one of the more drastic methods outlined earlier.

Exercise

Apart from the particularly drastic play techniques designed to cope with specific situations, there are a number of important areas where play also serves a very useful purpose apart from just giving pleasure, and one is the exercising of your humans. People need some distraction from their disorganised daily lives and their preoccupation with apparently meaningless rituals, and the responsible cat can do much to help.

Many cats will evolve their own techniques geared to the individual peculiarities of their own humans, but for the inexperienced people-owner it is useful to have some methods of a universal nature. Bearing in mind that agility on your part is a prerequisite of any game involving humans, and also bearing in mind the notorious clumsiness of humans, one useful general technique is the *wool game.* In this game the cat uses his natural stealth to approach the target unobserved, the objective being to gain possession of the largest possible ball of wool; a soft, string-like material which extends for a considerable distance.

Once this has been secured there are two methods of proceeding; either by carrying the ball securely in the mouth or, in the case of large spheres, by patting it along the desired course. Whichever one is considered appropriate, make certain that the path taken is as circuitous as possible and involves as much back-tracking and changes of direction as can be arranged. Wherever practicable, execute circles around obstacles such as tables and chair-legs, especially those supporting delicate or fragile objects, as this will guarantee the most enthusiastic human participation.

The appeal these games have for your charges will be very evident from the volume of noise they elicit, for humans equate enjoyment with sound and the more pleasure you afford them the higher the pitch of the cries they make. It is quite likely that they will become so enthusiastic about this sport that they will attempt to spur you to even greater efforts by hurling inanimate objects after you. There is no great risk that you might suffer any discomfort provided that you are reasonably alert and move swiftly from place to place. Humans sometimes indicate their desire to play this particular game by

fiddling with one end of the strand of wool with slender metal rods, the symbolism of which is not yet clear. It has been suggested that they are substitute claws indicating a wish to be viewed by cats as being one of them, a theory supported to some extent by the glee with which they respond to the games.

Further exercise techniques
Another useful exercise game is the Cat As Prey Game in which the cat presents himself in such a way as to arouse the latent hunting instincts present in every human; instincts which the human's social habits repress in a singularly unhealthy way. Triggering these instincts will not only exercise the minds of your people but will allow them to use those hidden reactions sufficiently to keep them in the peak of condition.

Try stealing food off their plates when their attention is distracted and you will see how easily these important instincts are activated.

Even better is the technique of jumping up onto the small tables or shelves where people tend to place small objects of spiritual significance. Your very presence

among these sacred artefacts, irrespective of the care with which you station yourself, will elicit a fascinating and immediate response. It is interesting to note that humans, rather like cats, will elect for one of two probable approaches once they have noticed your position. They will either choose to fix you with an alarming, wide-eyed stare intended to paralyse you with terror while rising slowly to a half-crouch attitude and creeping towards you with their arms raised in anticipation of seizing you, or will make an abrupt spring. The latter is often accompanied by a wild and blood-curdling shriek intended to achieve the same effect as the manic stare.

In either case it is important only to have encouraged this reaction, and once they respond you can retire gracefully out of harm's way with your objective satisfactorily accomplished. It may be necessary to vacate the vicinity for a short while as it takes a few minutes for the human's impulses to evaporate and allow them to continue their earlier activities. Do not repeat this ploy too frequently as they will start to take the matter too seriously and will begin to anticipate your intentions, or even to extend the hunting process to other times and places.

A more sophisticated form of hunting game for cats with some time to spare, is commenced by performing some suitable trigger event such as the spilling of milk, knocking one of the previously mentioned sacred objects to the floor, or by using any other means which experience of your humans suggests. You then retire to a preselected hiding place and await the discovery of your trigger. Within a short time, the human concerned will appear at the door and will begin the long process of trying to find you. An occasional dash from cover on your part will help to keep the game moving along, and will keep their enthusiasm at a healthy pitch. Eventually, however, they will tire and their retreat to the house is the signal that the game is over for the meantime.

Advanced games

For cats who have had their people for some time, there is always the risk that many of the standard ploys will cease to be novel and the risk of the humans going out of condition increases accordingly. It is at this point that a conscientious cat must resort to other means of keeping them healthy and active, and there are several techniques which can be employed from time to time to vary the routine and keep them on their toes.

The first of these is the *libation game.* For this it is essential to keep a note of the days of the week as human behaviour seems to be closely geared to particular 24-hour cycles. There is one day in every seven-day cycle which is set aside for various forms of entertainment not generally practised at other times. One of these is the pouring of water over the family motor car. This mysterious ritual is probably of deep religious significance and one of the most widely accepted theories is that the chief male offers a libation to the beast as a symbol of appeasement in order to ensure its co-operation and correct behaviour during the coming week.

They appear to derive great satisfaction from this ceremony, an attitude which allows you considerable

opportunity to join in the festivities. One game which seldom fails to afford them tremendous amusement involves waiting until they have reached the closing stages of the ceremony when the human is making mystical passes over the surface of the beast with a sacred fragment of cloth. Shortly after this stage of the ritual has begun, approach the creature from the opposite side and, waiting until the human is admiring the results of his efforts, leap lightly onto its upper surface and walk casually about.

As soon as he sees you there, he will immediately begin to play, and his enthusiasm will be apparent from the lively waving of limbs and raucous shouts. He will try to join in in his own clumsy way of flicking the sacred cloth at you, hurling small pieces of twig, etc. This procedure can be repeated several times, but take care not to interrupt the ceremony for too long as he will eventually resume his duties by hurling further offerings of water at the area where you are standing. This is the signal that the game should be concluded.

Morning exercise

It cannot be stressed too heavily how important emotional exercise is to humans in your household, and another advanced technique is the *start the day the playful way* method. This can be initiated as soon as the selected human appears in the kitchen to prepare food or drink. They are often low in spirits at this point of the day and will stand motionless before the stove or kettle, dressed in their sleeping attire, with an expression of profound sorrow. This trance-like state, like those discussed earlier, is not at all beneficial to their spiritual well-being and should be discouraged at the first opportunity.

To commence the game, approach from behind as quietly as possible, taking care not to be observed, as this will destroy the point of the game. When you have stationed yourself immediately behind them, stand on your hind legs and begin the claw-sharpening routine at the point where the thick outermost garment terminates and the thinner inner one is exposed. Responses vary considerably but usually begin with the eyes, which widen to a most remarkable extent. This intriguing phenomenon is quickly followed by muscular spasms and an enormous amount of noise. Humans, due largely to their size and poor co-ordination, can be dangerous when stimulated in this way, and it is wise to make a strategic withdrawal once these reactions have been initiated and the game is in motion. The progress can, however, be observed from a suitable vantage point until the subject has finished its bellowing. Do not be distressed by the intensity of the emotion expressed as this is quite normal and will result in the termination of the trance-like state and the resumption of more normal behaviour patterns and routines.

Human-owners will gradually discover for themselves that, as they become familiar with the characters of their people, ample opportunities for evolving your own games will present themselves and will give them and yourself a great deal of pleasure. The secret of playing with humans is to identify repetitive behavioural patterns or routines and seek ways in which the monotony can be broken.

The grass game

For example, these extraordinary creatures have a profound dislike for grass which they see as a threat to their domestic security. At regular intervals one of the family will venture out and use a noisy device to remove as much as possible of the offending grass from the vicinity of the house. Try concealing yourself in a suitable stand of uncut grass until the human and his machine are almost on you, then spring forth with a piercing wail and watch their reaction. After a few repetitions they will join in the spirit of the game and will stop and search every tuft of greenery in gleeful expectation before attacking it with the machine. Although it greatly prolongs the grass-cutting ritual, you can be sure that much of the drudgery of this self-appointed task will be removed for them.

In conclusion, try to remember that despite their plethora of obscure and repetitive routines, slow-moving

manner and lack of initiative, humans have not been entirely subdued by domesticity. Deep within them lie all the basic instincts that we ourselves possess and with careful handling and sympathetic encouragement, these qualities can be exercised and developed once more. Provided that you are conscientious and considerate in tending to these needs you will be amply repaid by their response, and the marked improvement in their demeanour and physical condition.

One word of warning, however. Do not overdo this encouragement of their more natural instincts as too much emphasis will cause them to revert to their wild state. When they devote the large part of their time to creeping round the house, eyes narrowed and searching and springing at you with maniacal shrieks whenever you are dozing, it is time to give the games a rest until their enthusiasm wanes a little.

4.

GETTING THE BEST FROM YOUR PEOPLE

Although the process must, of necessity, be a gradual one, your main aim should be to establish a routine which is both satisfactory to you and healthy for your people. Humans are creatures of regular habits and inclinations, but sadly incapable of organising their own lives efficiently. They are too often distracted by petty matters and unimportant events, and the inevitable disruption will make them nervous, unsettled and susceptible to a wide range of extraordinary complaints.

Human ailments fall into two fairly distinct categories; the emotional and the physical. Due to their highly-strung nature, the former is the more usual, but is, fortunately, quite easy to diagnose and treat. One common symptom is irritability—as demonstrated by a tendency to be short-tempered and noisy; shouting at one another at frequent intervals and, more seriously, at you. In most cases it is best to allow them to vent their frustrations and nervous energy in this way. It is far more serious when they become unusually quiet and withdrawn. This is most unhealthy and should be discouraged without delay. How you turn this inward brooding to the preferable outward release of dangerous tensions will depend on the individual human concerned, but many of the methods in the section on The Importance of Play will work well.

The lazy human

Look out particularly for a reluctance on the part of the ailing human to rise from its bed, as indolence is a sure sign of nervous disorder. If you feel concerned about the well-being of one of your people, and their behaviour during the day seems to suggest that they are suffering from nervous malaise, pay a visit to their bed chamber next morning at the time they normally rise. Station yourself near the head of the bed to watch for tell-tale eye movements. If the person continues to sleep, avoid disturbing them as their malady may be no more than the effects of fatigue, but if you see that their eyes are open you can be certain that they are only trying to avoid facing their responsibilities.

In this case you *must* take swift action before the malaise gets too secure a grip. Spring high in the air, claws partially extended, while emitting the most blood-curdling shriek you can muster. Aim to land on the upper part of

the human's head (marked by a thick growth of fur), then leap lightly away from the vicinity of the bed and await results. In most instances no further treatment will be required; the human will reverse the introverted nature of the malady, arise swiftly and enthusiastically from its bed, announcing its return to normal with roars of relief.

If the affliction is more grave and this technique fails to have the desired effect the human will probably have withdrawn to the imagined shelter of the bedclothes, burying itself deep inside the covers. A less dramatic and more insistent ploy must then be used. Place yourself at the opposite end of the bed and look for the bulges in the covers marking the lower extremities of the creature. Climb onto the bed itself, take up station beside the twin mounds and, using the minimum pressure necessary, bite either tip. There will be a muffled wail and the lumps will move swiftly to another part of the bed. Repeat the process as often as needed until the covers at the other end are finally thrown back and the patient hurls itself out of bed.

Remember that forced termination at such an advanced stage is a difficult and distressing experience for your unfortunate human and, as with many creatures in pain, they will attempt to vent their spleen on the nearest party, innocent or otherwise. As soon as you have checked the success of the treatment, therefore, leave the area immediately.

The health problem

It is more difficult to identify physical disorders, particularly as many of them will have similar outward manifestations as emotional ones, but you should always try to be on guard for them. For obvious reasons, it is impossible to try and treat physical illnesses yourself, and humans do, in fact, have their own impressively efficient ways of dealing with such problems.

Certain members of their species, in recognition of the common lack of physical robustness and susceptibility to a staggeringly broad spectrum of ailments, have developed considerable skill in caring for their fellows; potions, medicinal draughts, rituals and mystic rites all seem to play a part. However difficult it may be to ascertain how these methods work, there is little doubt that work they do, and cats who, despite our superior physical condition, fall prey to illness or injury would be well advised to consider availing themselves of this traditional expertise.

Humans, being so preoccupied with disease and ill-health, are only too anxious to take advantage of the skills of their medicinal priesthood and will be happy to extend this facility to you. The customary practice is for them to transport you to the healing centre where you will find yourself detained in an antechamber full of other humans and their owners. This is a sacred place for people, and they are required to meditate in respectful silence until summoned by their priest, so you should, out of respect for their beliefs, resist the temptation to enter into conversation with any other cats who may have brought their humans along.

Being such highly strung creatures, humans get extremely tense in these circumstances and the period of silent inactivity leads to an increase in tension. If you get worried about the degree of introspection occasioned by lengthy and unrelieved meditation, other people-owners in the room will be only too willing to assist in any attempt to relieve the atmosphere and will join enthusiastically in a free-for-all. It will, after all, help to occupy the minds of their own charges as well.

The poor health and physical constitution of most human beings, probably the result of overbreeding, makes the continual monitoring of their condition of great importance. As described elsewhere in this book, you will need to devise a number of ways to keep them physically and mentally alert. Without this constant attention they are likely to slide slowly into indolence and lassitude. Keeping them up to scratch need not be too much of a chore; learn to make use of idle moments as they arise rather than interrupt your own activities to attend to this duty specifically.

Start the day the healthy way

First thing in the morning is an ideal time to start the day's programme of conditioning for alertness. Lie under the human's bed until you detect movement above. Soon afterwards, amid much puffing and groaning, a pair of bare feet will appear on the floor nearby, or a hand fumbling for the curious artificial feet that humans are fond of donning. A swift and unsignalled swat of a clawed paw and you can depart to pursue your own activities, leaving your human wide-awake and fully prepared to face the day.

Try sitting quietly inside a cupboard that you know one of your people will soon use. It will not even be necessary to make a movement when the door does open; your silent and unexpected presence within, and your eyes within inches of their own, will have the desired effect. The result is particularly gratifying when the human concerned is carrying a load of dishes or clothes, as the bending movements they will be forced to make to retrieve these items from the floor is excellent exercise for those little-used muscles of the back and shoulders.

Encouraging the hunting instinct

One of the most effective methods of helping your people's alertness is to stimulate their own hunting instincts. Due to lack of opportunity, these have been allowed to deteriorate by the average human and their reflexes have suffered sadly as a result. This fact is illustrated with pathetic clarity in some family groups when they attempt to improve their chances by regularly scattering bait at certain places in the garden. Once birds, squirrels, field mice and other prey have become accustomed to this practice and are regular visitors, the unhappy humans are unable to work out the next step and, instead, spend long, frustrated hours staring in silent agitation as their intended prey simply devours all the bait. Remember that people are essentially pack-hunting creatures, so for the best results, wait until most of the family group have assembled in one place before bringing in a live mouse which you have caught for the occasion. After freeing the prey in the room, remain at the door to prevent the mouse escaping before your people have had a good chance of catching it. You will be able to keep a proud eye on the proceedings perfectly well from there.

It is highly unlikely that they will actually succeed in capturing the creature, as their skills fall very short of your own, and they may even seek to enlist your help. You can, if you think it expedient, make a show of helping, but try to let them have a good run at it first, however ludicrous their attempts.

At this point it is interesting to note how the pack instinct, so different from our own approach, operates. The adult female tends to become the pack leader whatever her usual role in the everyday context, and she will station herself at the rear of the action where she can enjoy a clear view of events, and screech directions at the male hunter. He will make repeated and impressive charges at the prey, taking swipes at it or hurling objects at short range in an effort to tire it out. The younger members of the family will, according to their age and temperament, either join in with the male or will also observe from the perimeter. This scenario will continue until a lucky attempt actually succeeds in capturing the mouse or the humans themselves tire. In this latter case you will have to seize the prey yourself. It is a sad reflection on the extent to which their basic instincts have regressed that if, by some miracle, they do manage to catch their prey, humans are at a loss as to what to do with it and will even carry the creature to the door and let it escape alive.

Circulatory problems

As, no doubt, you will have observed, humans spend a great deal of time simply sitting or lying around in a semi-comatose state. There is little doubt that their blood circulation suffers as a result; hence the importance of some of the shock tactics already described. If these tactics, for one reason or another, seem to be inappropriate at any given time, it is a good idea to use massage to keep their blood moving about in a satisfactory manner. To do this, simply climb onto one of the main body masses, make sure that you are comfortably positioned with your weight on your haunches, and, in a steady and rhythmic movement, press firmly with alternate front legs. Clench the paws as you complete each movement, partially extending the claws to prick the upper skin surface lightly. This encourages the movement of the blood through both the lower muscular layers and the upper skin surfaces. Purring softly at the same time will keep them relaxed and soothed until you have completed the treatment.

Bodily functions: a difficult topic

One subject which really cannot be left unmentioned is the delicate one of dealing with bodily wastes. It is an area about which human beings are peculiarly sensitive and, as the novice human-owner will quickly discover, can easily become the cause of acute domestic tension. So little is known about human psychology and behaviour that we can only guess at the reasons behind their attitudes in this matter. It has been suggested that it is, as with many aspects of human society, a matter of some mysterious religious significance requiring secrecy and solitude. I, on the other hand, am more inclined to believe that their attitudes are simply the result of a feeling of vulnerability.

The only reason for raising this matter is that it plays an important part in your people's attitude to your own functions. Enormous problems in your relationship with your humans will be avoided if you alter your own habits,

inconvenient though it may be. Your people will become intensely and irrationally agitated if you do not decide, for the sake of domestic harmony, to limit yourself to the garden and put up with the discomfort that this involves. You may feel that it is more than a little unfair that you should have to do this, whereas your humans do not. They do, however, have special places set aside for the purpose which, I can assure you, are singularly unsuitable for cats. If you try it, and misjudge your hold on the polished surfaces, it is extraordinarily difficult to extricate yourself because of the smooth and sharply curving sides.

Nocturnal rituals

The nights are one of the most difficult times as a direct result of human's inflexible attitudes in this area, and you may have quite a lot of work to do before you can gain control of the situation. If your people have not been owned before it is likely that there will be no egress from the house once the outer doors have been closed for the night, and you will be forced to undergo a tedious ritual every evening as they prepare to retire. You can do a lot to liven things up by playing hard-to-get which will lead to quite an entertaining chase game.

You can organise it as either a wild and exhilarating chase from room to room or, more subtly, a sophisticated game of hide-and-seek. Bearing in mind the fairly predictable routines favoured by humans, you can secrete yourself in some most unlikely crevice well before the 'ejection hour'. You will soon hear one of your people moving about the house in an increasingly restive fashion until they begin muttering. This is then abandoned in favour of outright bellowing which will continue to increase in volume until all the family becomes involved in the game.

Once the fun begins to wane, you can either make your way quietly and unobserved to the door to await one of

them, or alter your tactics in favour of the *room-to-room dash.* After some weeks of this ritual, it is very likely that your people will cease to be amused by it and will finally decide to provide you with your own doorway. Although this is generally a much more desirable arrangement, there may well be times when you miss the excitement of the chasing game, but do not despair. It will only take a small damp patch on a conspicuous part of the carpet to precipitate another spirited gallop round the house.

There will always be certain difficulties about owning people, the nature of which will vary considerably from individual to individual according to their natures, characteristics and degree of domestication, but there is very little doubt indeed that it is a rewarding experience. How much pleasure and service you manage to get out of them will depend entirely on the amount of work you put in. The effort you make during the first weeks, however tedious and demanding this may be, will govern the quality of your relationship with them, and skimping on these crucial early stages can have unhappy long-term consequences. There is nothing much that can be done to correct the behavioural patterns of poorly trained people once they have been conditioned.

The initial period will make great demands on your time and energies, but handled with compassion and firmness can also be great fun. Humans are, by and large, of a warm and willing disposition with a tremendous enthusiasm for loyal service. The object of training is, therefore, to develop and exploit these qualities while suppressing the wilful, inflexible side of their characters. Left to their own devices, people are inclined to be unpredictable, introverted and obsessed with their own obscure behavioural rituals; qualities which are entirely detrimental to the interests of a potential owner.

Owning people offers the caring cat a new and entertaining dimension to life; it is exciting, frustrating, sentimental, infuriating, exhilarating, confusing, altogether richer and, most important of all, a great deal more comfortable than life in the wild.

5.

A DAY IN THE LIFE

As a guide for the novice human-owner, I have set out below a useful typical daily schedule as a framework for early training. It takes into account most of the important and critical points likely to be experienced in the initial stages of ownership, but is by no means a definitive plan and can be modified according to your particular situation and needs.

Daily routine

7:00am—Climb onto adults' bed and pat heads with claws retracted. If this fails to arouse your people, repeat, using claws. Further action is seldom required. Retire under the bed.

7:10am—Await appearance of feet beside bed. Strike sharply to discourage sluggishness and stimulate circulatory system.

7:20am—In kitchen. Milk will probably be in evidence at this time. If none is offered, butt ankles of human with head repeatedly to stimulate feeding response. You can usually leave your people to their own devices for a while now, unless you have reason to believe that their emotional state is depressed. If this is the case it may be productive to introduce a game at this stage.

7:45am—If a game is required, wait for the moment when the human is preparing to place its back paws in its woolly bags. Rush in and seize one. The human will be happy to join in a healthy chase for several minutes. This will usually be sufficient to get him into condition.

8:15am—Other members of the group will soon appear to feed. You will be able to join in the feeding, particularly if there are young in the household. This promotes a feeling of unity.

8:45am—Some members of the group will now depart (to hunt?) so accompany them to the domestic boundary as an act of companionship. The female will probably remain.

9:00am—On most days, the next eight or nine hours will be yours to do as you please. Two days in every seven seem to involve all the family group remaining together all day, and I call these *group days* to distinguish them. Use these communal sessions to look for opportunities for constructive play. On ordinary days the female of the species often spends far more time at home and will, therefore, need to be entertained a great deal more. There is much to be said for concentrating on the training of the female who will then help to reinforce the behaviour patterns of the other members of the group. Her activities during the absence of the others will afford many admirable opportunities for play and instruction.

1:00pm—Human feeding-times are fairly regular, and it is worth co-ordinating your own meals with theirs. Not only will you reduce the risk of your own nourishment being overlooked, but you may enjoy the added bonus of being able to win some of their own food. This can be achieved by techniques such as direct appeal; head-butting, sidling and purring or lap-hopping or, more entertainingly, by stealth and subterfuge. This approach has much to recommend it. Apart from being excellent practice for you, attempting to remove your people's meals from under their very noses is an admirable way of keeping them alert and their reactions in fine fettle. It has its dangers, of course, but this is no bad thing and adds a certain spice to your relationship with them. It is worth devoting a little space to this particular activity so that you will be able to act swiftly when the time is right.

1) Feeding and provocation

Young humans are clearly the easiest targets as they have yet to develop the jealousies and self-interest found in more mature examples of the species. Apart from your own pleasure in supplementing your diet there is, therefore, only a minimum benefit to them in initiating a feeding challenge. It is a very different matter with adult people as they will have developed a strong protective instinct about their own feeding events, and this is clearly illustrated by the fact that they will not permit the taking of food even from each other.

To conduct a feeding challenge you must feel fairly confident about your own level of skill and fitness. Humans, though slow, clumsy and naturally quite benign, are capable of rage, and when aroused their enormous strength can represent a considerable danger to the careless or unfit cat. It is easy to become over-confident about your ability to control your charges, so always bear in mind the fact that, as with most primitive creatures, they can revert to their basic natures. When adopting approaches such as these you will often be testing your own physical prowess as well.

2) Mealtime phenomena

As we well know, humans have a powerful ritualistic approach to life and the feeding process is no exception. Meals are the focus of a clearly defined ceremony which takes place at more or less fixed times irrespective of actual hunger. The female usually prepares the food in isolation and will resent the intrusion of any of the others whilst doing so. Other members of the family group take their places at the table at her command and wait there until the food is presented to them. This is your cue to take up a position beneath the table. Once the meal is under way amid much activity and noisy communication, move stealthily to a position beside your chosen subject and fix your eyes on the area immediately in front of him or her. This is where the food is actually lying and this will be your target area.

There are really two main options as to your next move and both depend on swift and decisive action. In your favour is the fact that humans, for some reason which has never been satisfactorily explained, only devour their food with the use of metal instruments held in their forepaws. This means that they have to relinquish their grasp on these tools before they are able to do anything about intercepting your attempt to deprive them of their food. The first approach involves springing lightly, but with maximum acceleration, onto the lap of your target, then, with the minimum of delay, onto the table itself. Swing the paw in one fluid movement to scatter a part of the food on to the floor. Leap down immediately, retrieve as much as you can and escape, amid the deafening roars of your frustrated and shocked target.

The second technique is to fix your gaze where you estimate the food to lie. Carefully watch the paw movements of your target to get an accurate fix on the position. Once you are confident that you have its exact location firmly in mind you are ready to perform. Gather your haunches under you, fidgeting your hindquarters to get the best possible purchase, and hurl yourself upwards while reaching out with your forepaws. As soon as your head is level with the table, and the edge of the plate carrying the food is within sight, bring the paws down as heavily as possible on its rim. If your aim has been accurate, while you drop back to the floor, the whole plate will up-end itself in a most spectacular fashion to catapult its contents in an arc across the room. If you begin moving as soon as you hit the floor you should arrive at the bulk of the food at about the same time as it lands on the carpet. It is then a simple matter to scoop up as much as you can comfortably transport and make your escape from the room before your target has even raised itself from the seat.

Do not be alarmed by the activity which will follow. Your people will feel a strong sensation of anger at the capture of some of their food and shame at having been out-manoeuvred so easily. After a period of furious bellowing and rampaging round in search of you, they will gradually quieten. If you allow a reasonable period of time to elapse before putting in another appearance, there is even a chance that you may be able to repeat the challenge. Remember, however, that if you intend to do this, extra care will have to be taken as they will be more alert next time.

Despite my earlier statement regarding the rigidity of humans' feeding habits, you will possibly find that at certain times they will decide to vary the routine. This is an event most likely to occur in the evenings when they situate themselves in whichever room contains the box-comforter with the glass front, which they call the 'tv'. As they will be seated in more accessible positions this allows much greater opportunity for carrying out a feeding challenge. You will find that you are able to approach much nearer without being observed, and that there are more avenues for escape once the act has been performed. Incidentally, bearing in mind that you cannot repeat this exercise more than once or possibly twice in each seven-day period, it is worth waiting until the fifth day, since then the food is very frequently hot fish, and well worth a pounce.

Daily routine (continued)

2:00pm—During normal days you can devote most of the afternoon to your own affairs and take a well-deserved rest from your duties as human-owner. It means that you can take advantage of the absence of most of the humans to relax in peace in a way which is seldom possible when they are present. It is a good opportunity, for example, to do a bit of scratching about and dust-rolling in the area where vegetables or flowers are grown. This is normally quite difficult to do without the risk of interference from the male adult who often assumes some sort of personal responsibility for the growth of plants.

During group days, however, the luxury of undisturbed relaxation is a rare one; there are too many things which have to be done to keep your people occupied and active. This is the time for many of the play exercises described earlier in this book and you will be kept very

busy if you are conscientious about your responsibilities.
4-5:00pm—About this time you will notice a change in the behaviour pattern of your little group. As though by some mysterious telepathic process they will make their way quietly to the house from their various positions. The female will prepare certain liquids and an assortment of small votive cakes that I have found to be inedible. Humans, however, will devour them and drink the unpalatable liquids, and I believe this to be yet another form of penance. The advantage of this strange ritual is that it will give you a much needed break from your duties.
6-7:00pm—This is the end of the day's real activity. From about this time, the human brain having been active for the maximum spell that it is capable of, people slide into a pre-sleep period of partial coma. In moderation this interlude is vital to your people's well-being, but in excess has a mind-numbing effect. In view of the extraordinarily

limited mental capacity of the species, prolonged inactivity of this kind can only have the most debilitating results and may even cause irreparable loss of vitality.

Some mention has already been made of ways of controlling the amount of exposure humans have to the box-comforter, but there are other ploys you can utilise to keep them reasonably alert. One easy method which can be repeated as often as you deem necessary is simply to stroll into the room and station yourself immediately in front of this sacred box. Within seconds one or more of the people will make the effort to move you before settling down once more into their lethargic trance. Wait a few minutes then repeat the process. By alternating this technique with other, more drastic measures, you will maintain the minimum mental and physical activity levels essential to prevent the deterioration of your humans.

Some time during the next period, the humans will partake of their last feed of the day. After this they will probably return once more to their meditation positions, and there will be very little activity until the start of the retiring process which is staggered according to the age of the human concerned.

7:00pm onwards—By and large, your duties for the day will have been performed and you can busy yourself with your own interests and activities. There are, nevertheless, quite a few opportunities for various play exercises as your people prepare themselves for their sleep. It is at this time that you can witness the extraordinary phenomenon of pelt-shedding. For some reason people are unable or reluctant to sleep in their heavy daytime pelts and, piece by piece, they remove it to expose the horribly smooth and pale thinner one beneath. They will then quite often follow the ritual of submerging themselves in hot water. This is probably because the soaking helps to reduce the fairly considerable pain that they must experience as a result of peeling off the outer layers of the pelt. To protect the vulnerable underpelt, they will usually wrap it in a light pelt which is kept among their bedding in the daytime. The next day they are likely to re-equip themselves with a completely different pelt; this must create severe identification problems, for as any cat is aware it is almost impossible to distinguish one human from another without sniffing them.

The end of the human day

Once the humans are all safely ensconced in their beds, you can virtually stop worrying about them. Unlike us, they remain immobile for most of the hours of darkness and respond poorly to any attempt to engage them in play during this time. It is worth trying once or twice if only to make sure that they have not died during the night, but do not expect a great deal of enthusiasm for your games.

The only common exception to this long period of complete coma is the manifestation of the *nocturnal insecurity syndrome*. This normally affects only the adult male who, as the usual provider for the family unit, can occasionally become stricken with irrational doubts. These show themselves as an instinctive fear that the group's food supplies are threatened, and will encourage the adult male to carry out a check. This will involve an expedition to the kitchen, often performed with ponderous stealth, where he will open the 'fridge' in which much of the food stock is concealed. The feeling of insecurity is so acute that it will require the human actually to sample various items of the food therein to ensure that it has not been tampered with. It is invariably perfectly all right, but his relief at confirming this is often profound enough for this to be an excellent opportunity for picking up the odd titbit by appearing at the kitchen door and mewing as loudly as you can. The knowledge that you are there to support him with your cries will encourage him to share some of the food with you as further confirmation that it has not been interfered with in any way.

Standard variations: the seasonal exodus

Although people are creatures of regular habits, you must expect some occasional but significant variations in their routines. Every now and then they will allow themselves to become involved in a variety of activities outside the usual pattern of events. Once or twice during each seasonal cycle, for example, the whole family group will suddenly decide to abandon the home and vanish for a period.

This will occur at very short notice, but it is possible to anticipate the event some time before it takes place by watching for certain tell-tale signs. Look for a general air of restlessness and excitability, or preoccupation with piles of coloured paper covered with images of blue skies and large expanses of equally blue water.

The most significant clue is to be found a day or so before the exodus actually takes place. The female adult can be spotted pulling a huge selection of pelts from hiding-places and boxes with sliding compartments. These will be ceremoniously laid out in ranks, shuffled about, apparently rejected but retrieved again later on. Eventually, a final choice will be made and the favoured pelts will be placed inside a number of different-sized boxes with handles. These will later be placed by the male adult inside the noisy motor car that will be waiting outside to carry them away.

Unless one has no objection to being taken away from home and placed in an unfamiliar place in the company of a host of other unknown cats and lesser creatures, it is essential to watch for these signs and act upon them. The key point will be when the female is making her final selection of the pelts to be placed inside the portable boxes. This is the time to absent yourself from the house completely and you should already have located and prepared a refuge somewhere where your people are most unlikely to find you. You may well hear the intensive and increasingly desperate search that will subsequently take place, but harden your heart and ignore the frantic appeals of your people to return. After many hours, they will resign themselves to your disappearance and give up the search. Move to some vantage point where you can observe their eventual departure and, after waiting for a while to make certain that they have actually gone, you can return safely to the house. A human from another group will probably take over the role of feeding you until the return of your people from their extraordinary journey.

There has always been a tremendous amount of speculation as to the reasons behind this mysterious event. Significantly, it is known that most humans undertake this lengthy excursion at roughly the same time as their fellows. The most plausible explanation is that, in common with several other species, it plays an important part in their reproductive process. Young are carried for a long time, perhaps nearly as much as a year, so conception is probably an annual event. As a result of some primitive instinct, it is therefore probable that, when the annual period of fertility falls due, they migrate to their ancestral breeding-grounds where they remain until conception has taken place and then can return home. This theory is still unconfirmed, however, due to the difficulties of tracing the whereabouts of the breeding-grounds.

Standard variations: communal worship

Another phenomenon which occurs from time to time to disrupt the usual routine is that of *communal worship*. As we

know from our observations of the many strange rites and rituals which humans perform each day, they are endowed with a powerful sense of mysticism. This is most strongly demonstrated on the infrequent occasions when a number of humans gather together to perform certain quite clearly defined rituals.

In a typical gathering the start is marked by the clearing away of furniture by the 'host' family group. Small dishes of unappetising items of food are placed at strategic points around the room as offerings, and large quantities of appalling liquids are made ready. Once the preparations are complete, the adults will wander quietly around the empty room in meditation until the first outsiders arrive for the ceremony, usually in pairs. From then on there will be a fairly steady stream of arrivals until the gathering is complete.

As soon as the 'guests' arrive, outer pelts are removed and thrown into a huge pile in one of the upper chambers of the house, and each human is issued with a quantity of the sacred liquids which they are obliged to drink. Their containers will be recharged at frequent intervals throughout the ceremony. Later on they will also be invited to partake of a ceremonial meal, although this is not always the case. There seems to be no clear pattern to the precise form taken by the ritual gathering, but it generally involves continual vocal exchanges between all the participants, which grow increasingly raucous as the ceremony moves towards its conclusion. The noise levels are generally very high, often with a musical background.

The duration of the event does vary, but it can be of several hours and is obviously extremely fatiguing for the participants, as demonstrated by their unstable and more than usually clumsy gait when the time comes for them to depart into the night. There is little doubt that the ceremony is intended as a propitiation rite connected with the house itself; either to purge it of evil spirits or as an offering of thanks for the shelter it provides.

This theory is reinforced by a further ritual often, but not always, performed by the adult male after such occasions just before retiring to sleep. In this touchingly primitive rite, he pays his personal respects to the house itself by choosing one of the devices set aside for human bodily functions and, bowing low, or even kneeling down over it, calling out loudly in a curious gargling cry. This is repeated a few times before the exhausted male stumbles to his bed, confident that all has been done to ensure that the house will continue to give his family warmth and shelter. When your people have attended a similar ceremony being conducted by another family group, the male will often be moved to reinforce his appeal to his own house by performing again the shouting part of the ceremony in isolation on his return.

The dangers of participation

It is, incidentally, most unwise to attempt to participate in these gatherings if only because of the number of feet which seem not to be under the full control of their owners. If you are a trifle hungry, however, the considerable amount of movement and the preoccupation of the humans with what is taking place will allow some excellent opportunities for you to help yourself to some of the more appealing foods that have been prepared. If you prefer not to risk becoming involved with events and cannot face the distressing noise and general confused activity, you will still be able to find a most enjoyable assortment of titbits scattered on the floor once the room is empty and your people asleep. The kitchen will be piled high with used dishes offering another excellent foraging possibility.

These remarkable gatherings of people fortunately do not take place very often. I say fortunately because there is an inconvenient side-effect. Perhaps because of the emotional strain of conducting this energy-intensive ceremony and maintaining the incessant noisy vocal elements for the entire period of the ritual, your people will be particularly and unpleasantly out-of-sorts for most, if not all, the next day. The male seems to be especially prone to the stress factor.

The extent of the problem will be apparent as soon as the adult in question awakes. This will, in any event, be much later than usual and may delay your morning meal considerably. The actual point of awakening is usually marked by a low, blood-curdling moan of utter misery and despair. This and subsequent indications seems to suggest that your human is in the direst agony, though it has proved impossible to establish what can have caused him or her so much distress. Alternatively, it may be that this is still part of the previous night's ritual, but I personally do not subscribe to this view as the appearance of extreme pain is far too convincing to be so easily dismissed.

Most of the day for your unhappy human, particularly the early part of it, will be endured in uncharacteristic fashion. He, and possibly she, will devote the bulk of the time to sitting absolutely still. Little food will be taken. Large quantities of fruit juice and a noisome dark fluid will be consumed at frequent intervals and there will be much holding of heads in paws. The eyes will be curiously unfocused for much of the time and any movements will be unusually slow and deliberate. There is also a marked reduction in the noise levels and a great deal of whispering, hardly surprising in view of the vocal and auditory excesses of the previous evening.

This is not a good time to make your presence too obvious or to perform any of your usual training or games exercises. Your people will show little enthusiasm for the customary activities and are, indeed, inclined to be irritable and ill-tempered and can resent violently your interference. The wise and understanding cat will turn a blind

eye to this lack of obedience and apparent regression and would indeed risk injury by being too insistent. It is far more productive if you allow your people this brief vacation from their duties and responsibilities and wait until the following day to reinstate the normal routine.

In conclusion

I feel certain that any cat who has adopted one or more humans will not hesitate to endorse my view that it is of enormous mutual benefit. There are, of course, numerous difficulties involved in participating in what is, after all, a somewhat unnatural alliance, but I hope that this book will go some way towards helping conscientious cats overcome any of the problems with which they are faced. Human owning will, if nothing else, add a new dimension to most cats' lives and will ensure a full, active and usually very comfortable existence.